FROM GOD, FOR YOU AND ME

Angelic Dreams and Supernatural Encounters

BY MONIQUE A. EVERETT

Copyright © 2020 Monique A. Everett

All rights reserved.

This book or any portion thereof may not be reproduced or used in any manner whatsoever without the express written permission of the publisher except for the use of brief quotations in a book review.

Cover Design by Monique A. Everett and Patricia A. Wentz

Illustrations by Patricia A. Wentz

Automatic writing and sketches by D.L.

ISBN: 978-1-7352872-0-1 (eBook)
ISBN: 978-1-7352872-1-8 (Paperback)

DEDICATION

I dedicate this book to my mother for her faithfulness, my brother for his financial support, and my father for teaching me unconditional love. Plus: my lover, D. L.—your toughness, intelligence, and spiritual debates have been true channels to my success.

CONTENTS

Preface: Spiritual Suspension

January 10, 2013: My Divine Dream of Archangel Michael

Introduction to Spirit

June 2, 2013: Rise and Teach Love Again

June 5, 2013: Shards of Glass

June 7, 2013: Recreations

June 7, 2013: My Tabernacle

June 27, 2013: The Void

June 27, 2013: Questions for Spirit

August 9, 2013: Cry for the Living

August 14, 2013: Aphrodom

August 18, 2013: The Reveal of Aphrodom

August 22, 2013: Genuflect

August 23, 2013: Do Not Neglect the Sustenance I Provide

August 23, 2013: Divorce

August 23, 2013: New Beatitudes

September 3, 2013: The Oppressors Will Fall

September 19, 2013: A Millennium Is Too Long

September 25, 2013: Love Is a Sacrifice

October 6, 2013: Reflect on Your Dharma

October 11, 2013: The Yoke of Love

October 23, 2013: Offer Your Neighbor Help

October 24, 2013: Be a Good Heart

November 6, 2013: Blessed Are Those Who Teach

November 21, 2013: Progress

November 23, 2013: Money Is an Enhancer, Not the Answer to Love

November 23, 2013: Be Humbled

November 26, 2013: Help the Poor

June 4, 2014: You Are Worthy

June 6, 2014: A Basket of Peaches

June 7, 2014: Material Things

June 9, 2014: Display Your Agony

June 9, 2014: Do Not Fear Death

June 11, 2014: School Shootings

June 12, 2014: Do Not Distract Love

June 16, 2014: Care for Those That Cared for You

June 21, 2014: Give and Expect Nothing

June 22, 2014: Be Benevolent

August 10, 2014: Ants in My Colony

August 10, 2014: Do Not Desecrate a Consecrated Host

September 12, 2014: Feel the Pain of Your Brethren

September 12, 2014: A Crime of the Heart

September 21, 2014: A Silo of Hay

October 3, 2014: The Virus of Hate

October 11, 2014: Salt of Your Tears

October 13, 2014: Jesus Still Loved His Betrayer

October 16, 2014: Cooperation

October 16, 2014: A Prayer for Saving

October 16, 2014: Diseases

October 16, 2014: Pacify Hatred

October 16, 2014: One Good Person

October 17, 2014: A House of Gold

October 27, 2014: Karma of Bad Lovers

November 29, 2014: Know the Beatitudes

December 4, 2014: The Path to True Happiness

December 19, 2014: Feel the Blight of Cain

January 1, 2015: Compromise-Based Solutions

January 12, 2015: Walk the Mount of Beatitudes

May 29, 2015: Gifts to Inspire the World

May 29, 2015: Equality for All

May 29, 2015: True Leaders

July 16, 2015: Expose Corruption

July 16, 2015: Collective Heart of Love

December 14, 2016: Aleppo Was a Warning

December 14, 2016: Love Each Other Equally

December 31, 2016: True Channels

January 21, 2017: The Face of God

Parable One: A Woman Sits Alone

Parable Two: The Man with a Cane

A Personal Essay from Death

Conclusion

About the Author

FROM GOD, FOR YOU AND ME

PREFACE: SPIRITUAL SUSPENSION

I experienced a "dark night of the soul" for almost two decades and suffered blindly through years of spiritual suspension without heart. That said, I continued to go to work and practice positive mentorship of my students during this frozen state of existence. Yes, I'm a teacher, but one can always be a productive member of society while existing in an emotional state of nothing. Then, one night, I had a divine dream of an angel, absorbed the golden light of love, and emerged out of my spiritual suspension shining brighter than I ever thought possible. I was forty-three and had just encountered my first miracle. Little did I realize that more miracles in the form of divine messages would continue until this day—an experience I share here, in my first book, *From God, for You and Me: Angelic Dreams and Supernatural Encounters*.

JANUARY 10, 2013: MY DIVINE DREAM OF THE ARCHANGEL MICHAEL

I went to bed as I had for forty-two years, with nothingness inside of my forlorn heart, even though I was a teacher and tried to model good behavior for my students. But all of this changed, forever, after my divine dream.

—M.

My spirit feels empty as I walk through an exit door and into a parking lot. The lights go out. The door behind me disappears, and I'm lost. Darkness overwhelms me because I'm just a little girl. I look around for help but can't see anyone or anything. Then I hear bursts of loud cackles, shrieks, and yells echoing in the night. I'm petrified and hold my ears shut in a pathetic attempt to block out the noise. But the high-pitched sounds are still unbearable, like sharp nails scratching on old and rusted metal cars. So I cry and beg the darkness for the torment to stop. Unfortunately my tears only encourage the mockery of the unseen creatures hiding in the pitch black.

"Is this how my life ends, even though I believe in God?" I ask in disbelief.

Boom! A loud crack of thunder erupts above my head while my knees buckle. I look up and witness a large hole opening up in the dark sky.

Then white light emerges in the darkness and fills the dark parking lot. The unforeseen creatures scurry away from the light. Then two large feet and long, glowing legs step out of the hole in the sky and start walking toward me.

Archangel Michael by P.A.W.

Helplessly I watch a very tall man approaching me in the darkness. His skin radiates a powerful light, even though his sandals are worn thin. His shoes remind me of the sandals that Romans wore a long time ago, with laces tied up around the ankle and shin. His stance is very heavy as it crushes any unforeseen creatures trapped beneath his sturdy feet, like old cars getting smashed into tiny bits of junk. I want to run, but I'm too frightened to move. So I close my eyes, hold my breath, and clench my chubby fists while awaiting the end.

But the tall man stops directly in front of me. My eyes are closed tight, but I feel his powerful presence wavering in front of me. Slowly I open my eyes but only to see *two dark eyes* staring back at me! My eyes pop out of their sockets with shock, and I start to fall backward, but a sizeable glowing hand reaches out and braces my tiny shoulder. One touch from the tall man was all it took. Now a tranquil glow sweeps through my body, and his eyes appear as gentle as a dove's.

"You must be an angel," I whisper to him.

The tall angel smiles back at me with soft recognition. Then he reaches down, picks me up, and lifts me out of the darkness forever. Suddenly we are standing on a familiar road, Midway, where I grew up. My brother and I used to go sledding down this hilly road. The memories fill me with sweet happiness. Now the tall angel and I are walking down Midway. We talk for a long time, and I grow into a woman again.

The tall angel is wearing a short, flowing white robe. The only thing holding it on his body is a leather belt with a turquoise stone at its center. His brown hair hangs loose, and muscle lines protrude on his elongated arms. The tall angel has a pallid complexion, long thin nose, and bright lips that never move, even though I can still hear him speaking to me.

"What happens to our angels when we are bad?" I ask the tall angel.

"They simply leave," the tall angel answers with a slight shooing hand gesture.

"Does my brother have an angel?" I ask with curiosity.

The tall angel nods an acknowledgment and looks to his right. My eyes follow and witness a thick white cloud materializing in front of me. Then a group of feet appears, and the feet begin to shuffle beneath it. I see sets of sandals—fancy or plain, old or new. Then a pair of elegant, gold leaf shoes steps out from the white cloud, and a handsome gilded angel emerges before me. I cry with tearful admiration as his robust body shimmers with gold dust amid the glowing mist. Even his thick, shoulder-length hair appears highlighted with glamorous.

This must be my brother's angel, I surmise.

My Brother's Angel by P.A.W.

Then my brother's gilded angel nods at me in agreement before stepping back into the thick white cloud and fading away with the others. But my tall angel doesn't disappear. We sit on the side of Midway now, like deer resting at the edge of the forest. Then the tall angel raises his palms and beams light toward me. Instantly the golden light of love hits me, and it's almost too deep and inexpressible. But the power of God's love washes over me with emotional release, and all of my anger melts away. I feel at home for the first time in my life.

"I want to stay here forever," I announce.

"It's time for you to go back now," the tall angel replies.

"No, I want to stay here, with you, forever," I repeat.

"You have to go back now," the tall angel repeats as I'm floating away from him.

"But I don't even know your name," I ask and reach out to the tall angel as he begins to float away from me too.

"My name is Michael," the tall angel calls back to me.

"Don't leave me, Michael," I cry and reach out for him again. My divine dream was over, but not my life.

Suddenly I'm back in my bed, awake and full of sweat. I start to cry uncontrollably but with unconditional love for the world. It's a miracle.

INTRODUCTION TO SPIRIT

After my divine dream of the archangel Michael, everything went quiet for me from the other side—except my life. I was aware, busy, and teaching with zest again. After experiencing the light beams of golden love, I wasn't afraid of life anymore. So I started dating again and met D. L., who was different from other men. We loved each other the same, except he was tough, and I was reserved. It created a suitable balance, and we quickly became inseparable. Now summer was approaching, and I was looking forward to spending extra time with D. L. and writing again.

My ultimate career goal was to be a published author for children and young adults. I used to pray about it on my drive to work too. I had started a few books but needed big slots of time to complete them. So I was excited about summer break. Little did I realize my writings would expand my spirituality beyond my goals, prior understanding of the other side, and personal beliefs. And it all stirred wide open in my boyfriend's apartment, while I was making dinner.

"Stop ghost hunting and write for me," a firm voice from behind me said.

Slowly, I turned around from the stove, and there was my boyfriend, but it wasn't my boyfriend. This figure held my hands inside of his hands now.

"Who are you?" I asked, and my hair turned gray.

"You call me God, but I have many names. *I am Spirit*. Unfortunately no one listens to me anymore. Won't you listen?" God asked.

"Why me?" I asked with concern. "I'm not married, and I haven't been to church in years."

"You have a good heart," God answered. "It's hard to find a good heart. Won't you give me the summer and write the truth for me?"

"I will write for you," I agreed without further hesitation, which surprised even me.

"Then take off your shoes when you are speaking to me," God directed. "*I am holy*, and you're not."

So I kicked off my shoes, sat at the kitchen table, and began scribing for God. The first title, *Rise and Teach Love Again*, was written on little pieces of scrap paper that I often used for shopping lists. After the message stopped, D. L. went over to the couch and fell asleep for a long time. When he finally woke up, he remembered nothing of the supernatural experience. He even accused me of making it up, until it happened again and again between 2013 and 2017.

Over the next few years, I recorded sixty-four divine messages and two parables from the Spirit, along with one personal essay dictated by

Death. Some words were spoken face to face and others conveyed through text messages while I was teaching at school. To this day, D. L. remembers nothing, but I archived my handwritten papers and text messages from him to help substantiate each experience. It's important to note that I'm not a prophet or preacher but only a messenger. I hope you will listen too.

JUNE 2, 2013: RISE AND TEACH LOVE AGAIN

Human beings are my favorite creation, but you're doomed unless one of you rises to reteach love for others. Earth is my beloved planet. I saved my ideal world for my favorite people, but look at what you've done to it. You have ruined earth. Adam and Eve disobeyed me from the beginning. Even the holiest of holy men have disobeyed me. They have questioned me when they've suffered.

Don't you know? I created cancer and other diseases so that you would pray. I haven't created all of the natural disasters and such, but I will not intervene anymore. I will not send any of my own anymore either. I gave my only son to die for your sins, but no one listened. Still no one hears me.

Show each other love. If you do not, I may change my plans and not create Armageddon because I won't have to. Everyone hates. You're doing it to yourselves. So I'm just going to wait and watch you destroy each other. No one loves. I love you, but I'm angry. Everyone has a perceived image of me, but everyone carries hate in my name.

I have replacements for you if you don't rise and love me again. I'll no longer make men in my image. No more brains, eyes, noses, and mouths because they only make you hate one another. My new beings won't need them. Their energy will be enough. I'm only keeping the angels in my image, for they obey. So they'll remain.

JUNE 5, 2013: SHARDS OF GLASS

You can't break the leg of a chair and not expect it to fall. You can't break the law and not expect a broken system. You can't express anger and not expect riots in return. You can't break a glass and not plan to clean it up. You can't break a glass and not expect to step on it. An injury to your foot from a shard of glass may be slower to heal than one from a larger piece of glass.

JUNE 7, 2013: RECREATIONS

When I reflect on the soul, I see my birth in you. You're my painting of myself. Your different colors are pastels on my easel and parchment. I have painted your faces to be beautiful to me. Each one of you is beautiful to me. I gave you a brain to think, eyes to see, a nose to smell, and a mouth to taste. These are human things. You're my creation, and I love you.

I'm your creator and gave you a brain, but you have wounded me with your choices. I love you, but you have deceived me. Now I will feel agony for you unless you lay down your love before me and rise to love each other. If you do not, I have replacements waiting.

My recreations will consist of only energy. No brains. No eyes. No nose. No mouth. I'll recreate new beings without these human things because my new people won't need them. What would humans think without a brain? Would you taste the sweetest thing without a mouth and tongue? Would you smell God's flower without a nose? Love me as I have loved you, or I'll create anew.

Do you think I want to destroy and replace my creation, the ones I love so much? I have created all beings in all space and time, but none of my creations—old or new—have ever followed my laws. I love you, but you don't love and obey me. As a son over his father's knee, I will chastise and abolish you lest you rise to love me fast. If you do not, I will recreate you in whatever form I choose.

But I forgive when I feel loved by my creations. I forgave David and his sins. From David, I gave new rules. I gave earth my only son. Don't use the excuse of Satan. You've forsaken your love for me. So love me as I have loved you, or I'll create anew, for *I am*. I said that to Moses when he questioned me. Yes, lay down your love to me, truthfully, and I will relinquish my anger toward my children.

Recreation by D.L.

JUNE 7, 2013: MY TABERNACLE

Unholy men desecrate my tabernacle. They hurt my children. I don't even tell some religious leaders what I'm telling you because some of them are heathens. Heed this—when you take the sacrament from unholy men, your communion doesn't work. Everyone needs to hold hands and pray. Then I'll relinquish my anger over my children. We suffer, so we pray. Love is a gift. I forgive, even though forgiveness through my son was lost. I know who the liars are, for I can see all everywhere!

Unholy men are disgraceful, and I weep for them. You know there were only a few who ever truly loved me. You can name them, yet they have sinned. David was a sinner, yet I forgave him. I forgive when I feel loved by my creations. Do you think I want to destroy and replace the ones I love so much? When I look at my reflection, I see you. You're my birth. Lay down your love before it's too late.

Count the unholy that haven't laid down their love for me. Those who never curse me, I love. *Curse you. I am your father.* Show me your *love*! Yet I feel agony for you, as if you were an ant colony. I don't want to destroy you, but this time it will be permanent. Please hear me. You're talking to me. I tell you, I'll rid the earth of you and also my pain. Love me as I love you. If you do not, I will create anew, for *I am*. Yes, kneel to me truthfully. Don't get on your knees, then go out to curse me. I despise liars and unholy men who desecrate my tabernacle.

JUNE 27, 2013: THE VOID

I've created life before, but they're of other content. They're more intelligent than you. They pass through me without death. They destroyed and rebuilt themselves but not to my pleasure. I gave them the gift, but they hurt me just like you. So I sent them to the void, but you can't reach them with your technology. Space and distance mean nothing to them because their development is more complex than that of humans. They're of a different makeup and can jump. I send them to check up on you, but I love you more.

There's a connection between past creations and humans. Don't try to visit them because I won't allow it. Don't do your algebra because there's no math or time in the void. The void doesn't exist for humans. If the vacuum doesn't exist, creations of existence must take place for survival. How do you create? I only allow my creations to love. It's about me, not you. They've been and still are here. They and their hatred for destroying themselves created all of your false gods, like Poseidon. There's nothing in the void that I didn't create.

The void, time, and space are so close. Don't you see the connection? Math isn't necessary. There are no idols, only me. Do you know the myths you believe are false? I'm the only one. I will be angry with your disbelief. I've destroyed all of the giants of your past beliefs. Don't falsify me by misrepresenting with your caricatures of false gods. I'll ruin you vehemently if you attempt to draw my face.

    There have been people who have visited you from the void, but you must not lash out in anger. They'll not hurt you. You can't stop them. Do your best to be who you are. I have told you many truths. Soon I will be done with you, my tiny creation.

JUNE 27, 2013: QUESTIONS FOR SPIRIT

"Who is the Holy Spirit?" I ask.

"The Holy Spirit is my love for the world I have created, for all of my creations. It was there from the beginning. I created my son after my spirit of love. I love my creations so much I encompassed everything within the Holy Spirit of love."

"Where did you come from?"

"*I am*. I've always been here. I'll always be. The only forbidden thing is to turn from my love."

"How many creations have you undertaken?"

"I created all matter in all places at all times. Space is small for me. You're tiny."

"What happens to us after we die?"

"When you die, you pass through Death and come to me."

"Where is heaven? Where is hell?"

"There's *no* hell for humans. If you're not with me, then you go nowhere. I would never torture my creations."

"What if we're not a good person and commit genocide, like Hitler?"

"Hitler is no more. He's nowhere. Hitler was a teacher. I sent him to teach the world of hatred, but the world I created hasn't learned. My son was a Jew. Jews have suffered to teach the world a lesson about love. Hitler hated Jesus, and he was my son! But those who love come to me and only me!"

"Why do children get sick?"

"I've allowed sickness from the beginning. My creations must die. Children are the closest to me. If the world submits to me as a whole and together, my children won't suffer. Until then, I'll do as I choose. *I am. Do not question my ways!* My people are sad because they have not followed my love. Yet I love the people whom I created."

AUGUST 9, 2013: CRY FOR THE LIVING

Cry for the living and not those who have never lived. One has to be born and have opened his or her eyes to have lived. Upon opening their eyes for the first time, people see me. You won't remember me, but I will evoke you. Even babies who are born blind see me. So don't cry for babies who were never born because they have not seen me.

Babies who were never born go to nothing because they were never alive. But don't cry for them, for they do not hear your cries. Nothing ends in nothing. There's no consciousness inside of nothing. Don't you see it? Millions of babies die every day before they are born. So I have to send them to nothing because it's for their protection.

AUGUST 14, 2013: APHRODOM

There are three angels for you—one of enlightenment, one of knowledge, and one of the things that will occur. The first angel will awaken you, the second angel will allow you to understand, and the third angel will let you see. The first and second are here. The third has yet to come.

You must walk to a place of solace and think. When you come back, you will feel like a child. Walk to a place you feel unsafe. Stay until nightfall. Don't fear. Think as you have never thought. You'll be safe. Walk and don't be scared. Think and take solitude. Be sincere in your thoughts. Nothing will harm you. Go to a high point where you can see the beauty of all that's before you and touch the third one.

When you see the beauty before you, the third angel will rise and touch your finger. Then you'll see what will occur at the end. The third angel is named Aphrodom, and he's *large*! Aphrodom has never been allowed to reveal his vision, and it isn't enjoyable. He sits in wait for my command to tell it. Ask, and he will show the horror to you.

Aphrodom is an angel who has sat on a rock until commanded to reveal what will happen at the end. In the end, most will go to nothing because the perpetrators of the end will be the majority. Aphrodom is the only window through which those chosen can see what will occur. His rock is his seat until I give the command for him to get up, and he's enormous. Aphrodom will cause your eyes to widen in awe. Then he'll tell you the things you should do to save yourselves.

Aphrodom by D.L.

AUGUST 18, 2013: THE REVEAL OF APHRODOM

There's a tall, skinny white marble pillar overlooking everyone down on Earth. D. L. is standing on it but frozen with panic. His eyeballs are the only things that move to witness the death and demise around him. Disaster is everywhere. Volcanoes are erupting, and fires burn in the distance. Flash flooding fills the ground below him. There's nowhere to run. Everyone and everything will be dead. It's just a matter of time and how long you'll suffer before you die.

You're alone in the end. Screams like eagles crying pierce the sky under the wings of flames. There's nobody left to help anyone. Shades of red burn in the distance as people are eaten alive by the lick of fire. Dark waters below D. L. engulf screams to nothing. The end is a mirror that reflects only hate and its destruction. You die by burning, drowning, or succumbing to both.

It's D. L.'s turn to die now as dark waters rush up and around the white marble pillar. His feet are becoming drenched in rough seas. The wait for death is torturous, while his eyes swell with panic as the water rises. Imagine being the last person to see existence burn and drown as you suffocate inside of yourself. No one wants to die like this, but how do we save ourselves?

"*Pray*," the angel, Aphrodom, stands and announces.

D. L. prays and closes his eyes as the water rushes over his face. He prays hard for the souls of everyone who has died, especially his daughter. Suddenly D. L. is pulled out of the water and stands on a grassy hill. No more fires. No more flooding. No more screaming. No more end. Then he sees his daughter running to greet him in the distance.

AUGUST 22, 2013: GENUFLECT

Don't allow the teeth of the unrighteous to bite you! Never turn against those who've been unrighteous if they see the light of righteousness. Please don't turn your back on them, for they've laid down their arms for a righteous cause. Your enemy is your friend should he lay down his arms, genuflect on his knees, and surrender to the fair treatment of others.

The cold-blooded murderer can't genuflect. Killers can ask for forgiveness yet still go to nothing, for the cold-blooded murderer is negligible in the eyes of the Lord. Don't give up your cause of compassion and freedom because of fear; you may be too old or die before seeing the results.

Let's see what people are willing to give back in the name of their ancestors, who paved the way for their freedom. I bet those responding will be selfish, spoiled, and they'll forget about the relatives who dropped dead for them. Selfish people wouldn't sacrifice for their family, let alone their community. No, I curse the greedy. The selfish will enjoy earth yet see nothing.

AUGUST 23, 2013: DO NOT NEGLECT THE SUSTENANCE I PROVIDE

Your life would be more comfortable without me and harder with me in it. Eat my food. Drink my water. But do *not* neglect the sustenance I provide. Take every mouthful and drop. Don't spit it out. In your future, it may be sparse.

AUGUST 23, 2013: DIVORCE

The ramifications of divorce should be logically discussed in the best interests of all parties if a lot of money is involved. The man should be prepared to sacrifice a lot if he loves his children and trusts the woman who gave birth to them. She's the mother of your child, and the child deserves it. Mothers are the lifeblood of your child. Don't seek to escape that fact!

A man should know how important the mother is to the child and not avoid his obligation, unless she's an evil woman. In that case, the man should seek custody. Women take the advice of their mothers. No man can convince them as effectively. A man who doesn't listen to his mother will lose his woman, too, because he didn't heed his mother's advice. Some men won't take responsibility for their violent actions toward their wives and children. That isn't very responsible. Men who don't think before they act against their own family and abuse the mother of their children shall go to nothing!

I created the first man. After that, every man had a mother. How dare a man seek personal gain at the expense of his child? Gained riches are an accomplishment, not a right. How dare you not share with others in need? Don't you care for anyone but yourself? Why do you turn your back on others so quickly? Would you wash someone's dirty feet? You pretend to care. How many people do you think will believe you? I consider your falseness a sin. The sin against me is your desire to hate. Soon all may have the mark of Cain.

When I come again, all will see they've been wrong about me. Then the answer will be clear. Your question about what's wrong with society I will answer. You have killed in my name. Falsely you've killed each other in my name. Did I ever tell you to kill each other over me? No. I told you to love each other in my name. Remember, I'm the father and the mother!

AUGUST 23, 2013: NEW BEATITUDES

Everyone wants to give, but everyone's selfish. By nature, you want to give, but you don't listen to the saints. Saint Mother Theresa served as a lesson and sacrificed everything. Don't take but rather give. If you're not hungry, don't accept the plate. There's no reason to eat if you're not hungry. Give the plate to someone who needs it and don't take a bite.

Have you followed the Ten Commandments? Do you know the beatitudes? Answer me, though your answer will not be correct. A number of you will say you did. A number of you are liars. The most horrible thing is *greed* and your lack of compassion for each other. Here are the new beatitudes:

1. Blessed are those who have great thoughts, but woe to those who do not listen to or hear the worries of others.
2. Blessed are those who accept the Eucharist, but woe to those who don't taste the blood of Christ.
3. Blessed are those who see, but woe to those who are ignorant of the truth.
4. Blessed are those who submit to Christ, but woe to those who still want material possessions over love.

5. Blessed are those who built the tallest buildings to reach me, but woe to you who stop making steeples to find me.

6. Blessed are those who absorb the truth, but woe to those who still don't practice the truth.

7. Blessed are those who hurt, but woe to those who never feel the wounds of others before themselves.

8. Blessed are those who look to the future, but woe to those who never see the beauty of now.

9. Blessed are those who touch, but woe to those who don't feel the suffering of others.

10. Blessed are those who bend, but woe to those who don't bow before God, Jesus, and the Holy Spirit.

SEPTEMBER 3, 2013: THE OPPRESSORS WILL FALL

Holding your brother down and pulling the yoke from his neck while he lashes out is painful for him. The oppressors will serve the oppressed. The oppressed won't oppress their oppressors but will have mercy upon them and allow them to open their eyes from darkness. Then the oppressor will learn compassion and acceptance, like Paul.

The oppressors will fall yet be saved by those who value life over death. Then they will beg for forgiveness. If they ask with sincerity in their hearts, spare them. But heinous murderers cannot lie for their lives and will go to nothing in the end. The oppressors will accept a tyrant who spoon-feeds them the euphoric soup of hate. They will again seek to murder intellectuals who discard their beliefs as warped. These are the weak of mind. They have power in extreme ignorance.

Bullies, who seek power and not rational intelligence, will be ruled blindly and used by a leader who can destroy unless stunted by those who don't sit idle. The oppressors are wiser than you think and not foolish. They feel violated by the government and seek to conserve ideals that discriminate, which they see as proper. They'll not win. When confronted, the oppressors will cower. That's what a bully does because a bully is a coward.

The oppressors don't see their fight as violating the rights of individuals. They seek to conserve their rights to bear arms. They're so spoiled by freedom. They don't know the value of freedom, like a child doesn't see the cost of a dollar. Teach them appreciation of prosperity and choice, just as a child needs to know his parents worked for the money to buy his ice cream cone.

SEPTEMBER 19, 2013: A MILLENNIUM IS TOO LONG

A millennium of pedophilia is too much, but sadly the sin has been around this long. Let the guilty be exposed. No one suffers after death. Nothingness awaits the disgusting at heart. Jesus said pray in your home naked and expose yourself to me, for this is how it was in the beginning. You should wear a loincloth because of your shame and your sins. A building is not needed to worship what you feel in your heart. A foundation made of earthen material will eventually crumble and fall. Love is the binder. The self-admitted sinner is purposefully exposing the many wrongs of history. Do you think this is only a recent phenomenon?

The highest church has sat on a high rock, but the church will tremble with disbelief, and people will wander with mistrust for the church. Jesus never asked for this. So the leaders of the church must confess the sins of the church. The leaders know the church was allowing children to be hurt. The leaders must disclose the horrors of the church, repent, and accept punishment on behalf of the whole church. The leaders must take this fatefully.

The leaders of the church know they will be nothing and no repentance will please God, yet the leaders have come to acceptance enough to expose their compatriots. I tell the leaders that they are sinners because the church holds all humans as sinners, ever since the transgression of Adam and Eve.

SEPTEMBER 25, 2013: LOVE IS A SACRIFICE

Would you sacrifice your pinky toe for human suffering? If yes, then consider your toe sacrificed. The world cries but harbors your tears. Those who don't feel are hurting. They touch but don't feel. Listen to me. Don't speak. Your shoes are worn thin, just like your souls. Hark. Stop. Listen. If you do, I'll grant you understanding.

    Everyone is a sinner. So let your heart and feet beat on the same path. But I forgive you, just like a parent forgives a child. You must still answer to me if you've murdered. Believe my words. I'll always make you nothing if you continue to hate. Mark it. Never forget only I can pardon you.

    People of my lost creation should feel shame for hating each other. Yet I have hope and love for you. Show your true self. Sadness engulfs you because it is your nature to despise. Feel hate for its heartfelt reality, and you'll cry true love in your chest. You'll tear from the eye and bleed from your hearts. Love is a sacrifice, not a reward.

OCTOBER 6, 2013: REFLECT ON YOUR DHARMA

The earth changed shape many times before you. It has nothing to do with the conscious existence of your soul. There's no such thing as earthly. There's only a nonphysical experience, in which your body represents your image of consciousness. Intelligence does not recognize it yet.

If only everyone thought about Saint Francis of Assisi or Saint Mother Teresa, but no one talks about him or her anymore. Shame. Reflect on your dharma. Then walk, speak, and knock on doors. Spread love, kindness, and compassion. Lead by the examples of Saint Francis of Assisi and Saint Mother Teresa.

OCTOBER 11, 2013: THE YOKE OF LOVE

Parents always come first, for they loved you enough to put you first before all. Don't forsake your parents when they're old, unless they are corrupt. Listen to their words, for they have given birth to you. You must assume the yoke of love; although it is a burden, you must still do so.

There will be *no* solace for you if you forsake your parents and force discomfort upon them. A lack of love for one's parents is equivalent to being a viper. One may love not, but not loving is a horror to you and all those around you.

OCTOBER 23, 2013: OFFER YOUR NEIGHBOR HELP

Please don't sell your soul for lies. It's not only the responsibility of the church to care for those in need; you bear a responsibility to your neighbor too. Don't go to church and listen if you don't hear. Don't take communion if you feel separate from my teachings. That's blasphemy.

When you approach my tabernacle, don't think for a second I don't know the truth in your heart. On the Mount, you worshipped Baal and other false deities for self-pleasure and delight. Shame. I don't punish, but nothingness is forever, and you'll never be reborn. The uncaring and unloving approach me, but they're excrement.

It's not difficult to offer your neighbor help. One should never take advantage of assistance; instead, use the gesture of kindness to inspire the strength to move ahead. Should you forsake this offer and not try, your days will be difficult.

Please don't ask for the truth unless you want to hear it. Some will ignore the facts because they are vipers. Do you remember the fact that all empires crumbled when rulers oppressed their people? None survived.

OCTOBER 24, 2013: BE A GOOD HEART

Don't sacrifice good love for lousy love. Rid yourself of the person and the pain before you suffer a horror to your mind or body. You deserve better. Those who love you—such as your family, your husband, and your children—would do anything to help you.

Don't let your heart separate from your soul for anyone who seeks to deceive your kind heart. Don't fall prey to the fangs of lies and betrayal, for they'll bite you. Let those who truly love you guide you toward trusting love again.

A kind heart is the best. The good heart needs to beat with other good spirits. Help the wicked hearts understand and overcome their corrupt ways by remaining a good heart.

NOVEMBER 6, 2013: BLESSED ARE THOSE WHO TEACH

Blessed are those who teach, for they are genuine and will usher children to an awareness of the Lord. Don't ever go to church or any house of *God* and pretend to be what you're not, for you're in more significant trouble if you do than if you never step in my house at all. We still hear the teachings of Jesus today, yet no one listens. The government punished Jesus, and he was the best teacher in history.

NOVEMBER 21, 2013: PROGRESS

God created your brain not to regress but to progress. Fear not in the name of knowledge. Fear not in the face of fear. Fear not. You fear. You have fear. After all that I explained, you still fear.

NOVEMBER 23, 2013: MONEY IS AN ENHANCER, NOT THE ANSWER TO LOVE

Is your heart meek? When your lover puts wealth and greed over you and your offspring, then you're in love with someone who can't love you. Money makes wives hate husbands and husbands hate wives. Husbands and wives hate each other if they don't recognize that money is an enhancer, not the answer to love.

NOVEMBER 23, 2013: BE HUMBLED

Be humbled. To rely on your neighbor for sustenance is to have no regard for your neighbor's survival. You should help your neighbor because that's what you should do, but those who grope for help in an intruding and offensive way need to learn how to humbly ask first.

NOVEMBER 26, 2013: HELP THE POOR

Help the poor. I'm sick of people who pray and pretend yet won't help the poor. No worse than vipers and liars. When did hypocrites and vipers decide it was okay to attend church and pray but not help the poor and homeless? Didn't Jesus teach you to help the poor and the sick?

To go to church and pray is a lie if one doesn't follow the teachings. Lying in the face of God in his own house is a huge sin. Do these hypocrites listen to the sermon? These fakers are the evil ones. These liars and bloodsucking fakers who dare step foot in church are against the teachings.

After all of these years and education, one would hope people would be enlightened, but they are not. Jesus said to help the poor and sick. Most religions say to help the poor and ill. You are a heathen amid humanity if you go to church and then go home and do nothing to help the poor.

The pretenders pray to God but do the opposite. God teaches you to feed the poor and help the suffering, not the reverse. Hypocrites. Vipers. Jesus would call them hypocrites and vipers to their faces and turn tables over in church. Pretend Christians.

Most Christians today are the same hypocrites and vipers whom

Jesus spoke against in the Temple when he turned the tables. Worse now. They don't heed the beatitudes. Feed the poor or stop praying. Help the suffering or stop pretending.

The Lord did feed the poor with loaves of bread, and he'll never stop feeding them. Only greedy vipers forget to help the suffering. My answer is to give to, support, and love the poor. When we stop helping the poor, we're no longer human.

Christians need to recognize assisting the poor is what the Lord and Jesus Christ did. Giving without receiving is what you need to do to believe. Help the poor. Help the suffering. I need not say more.

JUNE 4, 2014: YOU ARE WORTHY

When you stop considering your values as a good person, you give up on yourself. I need you to know one thing—you are worthy. I have never asked anything from anyone. All I want for you is to love and be happy. I don't care how or where you live. Use only the bare necessities. I have been at the top and bottom. I have seen the light and darkness. I have laughed and cried. A hungry person who needs a mouthful of food should eat. A starving child who needs milk shall drink. Don't be ashamed of feeding anyone because food is needful sustenance.

A mother who does not feed her child isn't a mother. You'll feel worse in the end for not feeding your child than if you had fed your child. Every supper is your last supper, and no one should eat without an embrace of those whom they love. You should drink the wine for everybody, not just for me. I stand for everybody. Don't deny yourself the right to take the Eucharist. Communion is not even denied to sinners, for I forgave Mary Magdalene. You should forgive the transgressions of others because I love you. Hurt me. Burn me. Whip me. Hang me. Nothing will ever stop me from feeling the love I feel for you.

Nothing should ever stop you from feeling love for each other too. You may think God is a wonder, but I'm not. I'll never be a giant unless it's your will for me to be. There's only prosperity in the comfort of your own home, with people who care about you. Be old, sick, young, or beautiful, but you must sacrifice and care for those you love. Give to me with no delusions of grandeur. Forgive me, for I have accomplished great things in my life, but nothing could compare to the greatness that I failed to achieve with you.

All children are born of innocence and love each other. Give into the mind-set of loving like a child. Children have no comprehension of hate. When puberty hits, children start to dislike each other. That's when the influence of others impacts us. Patience with your child is worth more than patience with yourself. When you feel shame about another person and no hurt for your wrongs, look inside your heart. Then feel the horror.

Until bad feelings for the human race are no more, you can't love each other. All you can do is put up false smiles and know your intentions to be good or bad. Don't hide behind the curtain of God. I won't stop you, but I'll let you succumb to your own devices. One day people will have to show how sorry they are for the bad things they did toward each other, but no confession will save them from justice before they die. Their deaths will mean nothing to the children they deceived in their lives. The deceit will last for generations, and they'll have to live with the mark of their parents on their foreheads forever. If children disavow their corrupt parents, I forgive them, even though people will always know what their parents did.

JUNE 6, 2014: A BASKET OF PEACHES

A child's birthday party holds no prejudice. If adults thought like children, they wouldn't hurt each other. The Lord dislikes you more for disliking each other than for liking him. Children are parents, and parents are children. Together, they raise each other. Your time has been less than a day in my presence. If you mill your logs and build your house, don't expect the wood to last longer than family love. Your home may fall, but your house will still stand.

Remember, God has no gender. I created you through love, not copulation. You don't need physical stimulation to feel true happiness, like that which I feel for you. One day there will be a person carrying a basket of peaches. The basket of peaches will never be empty, and everyone will have a peach. A young boy will be holding the basket of peaches.

JUNE 7, 2014: MATERIAL THINGS

Those who give nothing and expect everything will get nothing. Those who give everything and expect nothing will get everything. If you want material things over love, don't expect anything. If you seek love over material things, then you'll receive love, happiness, and everything else that you need. If you race to the finish line, don't be discouraged by not winning, because love is the biggest prize you can ever win.

There's only one human heartbeat, and that's the beat of the human heart. A woman is your mother, and your father is your shield. Even the largest man suckled on his mother's breast for milk because that's what he needed. When the gladiators died, their mothers still cried over the deaths of their children. They didn't run away and hide. When you lash out toward the people who love you the most, you're only destroying your soul.

Don't chase away the ones who love you, or no one will be there to lift you after your legs fail. If you turn away from love out of selfishness, you'll never be loved nor be able to give love. Serving your gratification is the only way selfishness survives. Serve someone over yourself, and wash the feet of another. Then witness your selfishness being extinguished before your own eyes!

Choose not to take a selfless path, and you will see your selfishness become your seed of destruction. You will be sickened by your demise, and there's no cure for it. Do not fish for anything that will not fight to shake your hook. If you catch a bottom feeder, your hook will only stick.

JUNE 9, 2014: DISPLAY YOUR AGONY

The more one gets by way of selfishness, the more one will lose. There's no light when you suffer in the darkness of your transgressions unless you lay down and display your agony. Only the selfish refuse to take a sponge in hand and wash the feet of the feeble. But only the feeble will wash the feet of the selfish. The feeble are the ones who know what they should do. You must clean and help the feeble too.

JUNE 9, 2014: DO NOT FEAR DEATH

There's no wisdom or knowledge in death, but your soul will wake up. Then your actions will determine if you will sleep again in peace or live on earth again with love. There's no consciousness in death. Don't fear death for any reason. Don't avoid dying for those who love you and those whom you love. The meek will be the successors of earthly love, for they are the ones who have suffered at the hands of tyrants yet still forgive their oppressors.

JUNE 11, 2014: SCHOOL SHOOTINGS

The uneducated inheritors of wealth see schools as a daycare for their children, displacing parenting so they can get pedicures. In turn, their feet look stunning, yet mold grows under their children's toenails.

JUNE 12, 2014: DO NOT DISTRACT LOVE

Sodom and Gomorrah are destroyed because of overindulgence in selfishness and people turning their backs on God, not because of their sexual preferences. More people will create life than not. Do not worry about the end of creation. Within every man and woman, there's more than individual survival. There are living organisms within living organisms. Those who take the initiative to detract others from loving are causing their ability to love to die.

JUNE 16, 2014: CARE FOR THOSE THAT CARED FOR YOU

Those who cast away their bearer have no problem forsaking the ones whom they bore. If you can't care for those who cared for you, how can you care for those who need your care? When you care more for yourself than others, you take away the nourishment from those who need you. Those who need you will suffer while you indulge in your pleasures. As you seek the moment, you're neglecting those who need you for their futures.

When you give to someone, you'll live a lot longer, and your body will sustain itself much longer without food or water, than someone who only gives to his or her desire. On your deathbed, there's more pleasure in knowing you've provided for others than in only haven taken from others. This is what will make you brighter before your last breath, and you won't feel so cold.

JUNE 21, 2014: GIVE AND EXPECT NOTHING

For some, selfishness is too tempting. Love is too much of a yoke and too much of an effort for a childish mind to bear. Having a good heart means giving without receiving. Give, and you will receive the fulfillment of giving. Expect nothing in return.

The last vision the mentally competent will have before dying on their deathbeds will concern whether or not their obligations were fulfilled. Come to church not in your best clothes but your worst. Don't hide in the best robes of silk nor demand the best seat. Don't press your pants or wear makeup. Clothes can't cloak what you sincerely ask for with prayers. Pray naked in a closet in silence and fervency. That's meaningful.

JUNE 22, 2014: BE BENEVOLENT

The love your parents had for you as a child is the same love you should give back to them when they are old. Their knowledge surpasses every ounce of effort you could ever give back to them. Unless they are corrupt and abusive—then they have never given an ounce of energy, even unto themselves. It's the unspoken truth, yet well known.

For those who suffer in righteousness, the cup of suffering must remain for the sake of righteousness. Therefore the righteous must suffer. The selfless find it easy to live on so little, and the selfish find it hard to live on so much! One can be the happiest with the least and unhappiest with the most. The ones with the most can be happy if they think and feel for the ones with the least before thinking of themselves.

The gift of having the most is being compassionate and benevolent toward the ones who have the least. Even the destitute can give tithes—if not with riches, then with comfort and help. Hugs are worth more than wealth. Children need hugs before all things. Put yourself before others, and you will reach heights unknown, but your building will crumble for lack of solid foundation. Then your children will bear the weight and wallow in the rubble. Be benevolent.

AUGUST 10, 2014: ANTS IN MY COLONY

The world today has angered me more than pleased me, and I want to be happy with you. Remember, you're ants in my colony. I could swipe you with my foot and render you useless in one second, but my compassion for you prevents me from swiping you away.

Unfortunately "love" is the word I don't see much anymore. Based on your history, you're not good. I hope my creation survives and I don't have to destroy you as I have created you. Now heed this, I *can* end your life faster than I created you.

The person I speak through has not pleased me and isn't a prophet. I chose him because he has the will and strength to fight for life and love. He has done so, but don't think for one minute that this person is a prophet, for he's not. The person is an ant in my colony and one that I have chosen at random.

AUGUST 10, 2014: DO NOT DESECRATE A CONSECRATED HOST

All have sinned. All are willing to cast the first stone; however, your false innocence is treacherous. Don't shake your neighbor's hand in church until you're shaking your hand from your heart. Good people are willing to accept each other regardless of race or color. When you look into your neighbors' eyes and shake their hands, you have an instinct that tells you whether they're honest or not. Trust your instincts. You need to look into a person's eyes, and then you'll know.

Those who don't feel love for humans shouldn't take communion with the Lord. If they do, they are liars. Don't desecrate a consecrated host by the falseness of your own heart because this has happened too many times and isn't pleasing. The same goes for clergymen and those who represent God in my religion. Don't defile God in the heart, then give Holy Communion.

When you learn to love again and haven't committed crimes against humanity, you'll cry tears. If you don't mourn those tears, you'll be nothing, which means you'll die before your time. You shouldn't try to reason with your anger and hatred, for it makes no sense. The ones who die the youngest have giant hearts. I take them before corruption engulfs them with hate.

Did you forget how your mother treated you with love, kindness, and compassion? If you had no mother, I was there because I'm the mother and the father! Your comfort is through me because I'm your parents. It's my nipple you drank your milk from, and I'm the one who raised you. *I am* and will always be.

SEPTEMBER 12, 2014: FEEL THE PAIN OF YOUR BRETHREN

Until you walk across sharp gravel without leather from animals that I have provided for you to protect your feet, you haven't felt the pain of your brethren. Don't expect anything from anyone for your kind efforts because good efforts should only be from your heart.

People will seek to destroy your good efforts, but don't doubt yourself when you have a good feeling from your heart. Kindness will be recognized. You may face death for your kind efforts, but it will take a lot more than killing you to change what I have proposed for the ones who destroy.

People who put wealth, desires, and indulgences before their children, who need them, haven't heard my truth. There'll be no rainbow for you if you put yourself over the ones that love you most. I promise you that I don't condemn those who prosper but only those who put prosperity before their family or loved ones. The selfish will feel the worst in the end.

You bring horror and death upon yourselves. I never expected this from you. The Holocaust reflected your transgressions against the Jews. My son was a Jew, and you mistreated him. Cruelty against the Jews has revealed hate from the beginning.

When Cain committed murder, he couldn't control his anger and hatred for his brother. But I created all of you as brothers and sisters who should love each other in the same way. There'll come a day when I'm over you, but I won't sacrifice people anymore. I won't send my son as a sacrifice for your sins again. Instead I will hold you by the shirt collar and ask you about the evil things you have done! No matter what you say, you can't lie to God. I'm everywhere!

Don't picture a devil with horns, for I'm a worse judge of you than he could ever be. I already condemned him to hell. I won't torture you, but you'll go to nothing. Only the fallen angels know hell. I made them more powerful than humans and gave them the ability to make decisions. Angels live, but they're not human. They don't eat or expel excrement. Some are good, and some are bad. I favor the good ones, and I can quickly destroy all angels, creations, and the entire universe should I make that decision.

Yes, there's a hell for evil angels, but not for humans. There's no hell for humans because I love you too much. I love you because you're my children. I will continue to love you like a father and mother love their child. I'm putting more demands on you now than ever before because you should know the consequences of your past actions. I love you, but I haven't been pleased with you for over five thousand years now. That's a long time for you, but a short time for me. So I hope you'll learn to love each other soon.

Humans are born of innocence. Show me someone who doesn't love a baby. Show me a person who wouldn't protect a baby, and I will show you a person whom I cast out, like an evil angel cast out from heaven. All humans are equal. I love my creation, but I'm not shedding tears for you anymore. Now I feel anger. Stop indulging in selfish pleasures, and begin to follow the word of not only the Christian religion but also all religions.

I am the dominant and created everything. Your lives are a ball in my hand—I love you, but you're not the only one. I must tend to others too. If you learn to love each other, then you'll be like a classroom that doesn't need my attention because you'll be following the rules of success that I have planned for you. Remember, I'm the Father. I need not hang on the cross. I need not suffer for you. If I had not blinked my eyes, your world wouldn't have come into existence. I'm the Father, for I have created all of this for you!

SEPTEMBER 12, 2014: A CRIME OF THE HEART

I created sex between two people for love, not for hostility and anger against those who don't deserve violation. If you can't look your lover in the eyes with passion and love, you're committing a crime of the heart. If you take the vile step to penetrate someone without equal consent, compassion, and connection, forcing yourself on another against her will and to her horror, you rape yourself too.

Nowhere have I ever said to rape another human being or have sex with her against her will. If you commit such a crime of the heart, you must face the consequences and punishment. If not, don't ask or expect forgiveness. Don't misinterpret my words and use them as an excuse to violate someone. Anything I have ever said, from the beginning of Genesis up until now, indicates that your wife, the mother of your child, or any other woman you may be interested in deserves love and compassion equal to those of Jesus for Mary Magdalene.

SEPTEMBER 21, 2014: A SILO OF HAY

There was a drunkard, and his only job was to protect a silo of hay. He may have been a drunk, but all he worried about was the hay. He was the keeper of the hay. In turn, the hay fed the animals on the farm. The animals trusted and spoke to him, even though he was a drunk.

Stop focusing on others and start focusing on you. Those same animals that trust a drunk look at you with a mix of trust and fear. Don't judge. The drunkard fed the animals, but you waste the animals. You're no better.

Look at your table and waste. You're a spoiled glutton compared to the drunkard and his silo of hay. How much of this bone, meat, and fat could you have shared with someone instead of gorging on it or throwing half of it away? How many empty bowls could you have filled with one of your dishes of food? Feed the hungry and be like Saint Francis of Assisi. He gave up wealth and survived on practically nothing in order to live the life of Christ. He cared for the animals and still fed the poor.

Saint Francis of Assisi had compassion for animals just like you, but you must separate your emotion before the slaughter from the need to sustain life. Birds don't care for what they eat and have no compassion for the worm. They must survive and feed their babies. Mind you, I gave you animals to eat, but I never told you to abuse them. That's why you must bless and hug animals before they die. Then you will not eat their fear. Eat fish, meat, and fats, but don't waste the animals.

Save all excess, and feed starving people with it. Please don't make it about politics! Charity is a helping hand, not collecting tax credits. Did you know people are so hungry that they're eating excrement? Some are taken, raped, and abused. Captors take their food, and they have nothing. They eat dung while you waste your food. I would rather you be a drunkard guarding a silo of hay than a spoiled glutton and waster of animals.

OCTOBER 3, 2014: THE VIRUS OF HATE

The virus of hate and prejudice will destroy more than any other infection on Earth. When you put evil thought and intention before loving others, the virus of hate has infected your soul. Have you no lamentation for the poor, sick, and destitute? If you don't cry for others, then you are of evil thought. The righteous person who loves will always prevail.

Militant and violent religious groups that spread hate are selfish terminators who have misinterpreted the word. They are greedy conspiracists and feel only a false identification with love. Their caliphate is invalid. A false caliph is unrighteous and a murderer of his religious text. Choose? You either love or hate. Those who have joined evil have made themselves dirty and unclean. No virgins are waiting for them. *Never.* They need to beg now for forgiveness, while they're still from this world.

Those who hate will be hated, but you have brought this upon yourself by rejecting love. I have a place for Cain, the murderer of his brother, where the unforgiven receive no benefits from me. No human goes to hell; however, the murderer's punishment is being denied the prosperity of happiness forever and having to watch others be happy. I allow you to change your path before it's too late. You're low and nothing before me. I'm not pleased with your thoughts and actions. You don't even show any love for my son, whom I sent.

OCTOBER 11, 2014: SALT OF YOUR TEARS

Let the salt in your tears awaken you. Let the salt in your tears be reminders of why you cried in the first place. When a tear drops into your mouth, taste it on your tongue. The salt of your tears is distasteful to you. You can't drink a full glass of your tears without becoming ill because the salt from your tears is the poison of sadness.

Turn sadness into happiness. Seek fresh water and cleanse your sorrow. When your tears dry, you'll feel better. The goal of humans isn't to feel indifferent but to love each other. When tears fall, let it be a sign that something's wrong. Don't be mad while looking for answers from God. *I am* and want you to feel the sting. One taste of salt from one teardrop should be enough for you, as a creation of mine, to not want to thirst for the ocean.

The water of the sea is poison to you. It's a warning about where you came from. Let the taste be a reminder that you can no longer process it. If you were to collect all of the tears from everyone in the world and put them into an urn, would you drink the contents? Would you take even one sip? One sip may hurt you. Are you willing to take the pain of everyone's tears into your mouth? If you don't, you will be ignorant of the problems of the children I created.

Those who take a drink from the urn of tears will be closest to humanity. If you don't stop hurting each other, my tears may destroy you, for they are saltier than yours. Only one drop of God's tears will end you and the precious life I gave you. Jesus died at thirty-three and gave you decades of his experience.

You have lived decades, too, and that's why I talk to you. You deal with excrement, shame, embarrassment, and ridicule. These are things that I suffer with you, but don't consider your life special. You may feel euphoric in all of this knowledge, but I can still end your life tomorrow. Why have I chosen to speak through you? You don't need anything but love. You express your gratitude but expect nothing. You're a sinner, but you have a good heart. You drank the salt of tears from the urn, even though you felt the sting of sadness.

After you taste the salt of tears, you'll awaken! You'll come out of the delusion of lies! You'll realize that I still love you, even though a father must have anger toward his children when they fight each other. When you disregard morals that I taught you, I must punish you. I have brought you up like you should be bringing up your children. If you do not bring up your children with morals, you have ignored my teachings.

My teachings follow all churches, temples, mosques, or any religion in the world that teaches love. Believe in my love. I only hope you will take my advice before it's too late. Remember, there's no hell. There's only nothing, and nothing is still salty. Be a better person. Have a good heart. First of all, have the right mind and love those who don't. Measure up to the standards that I taught you with zeal.

People need love. So love them. You write and speak well, but don't forget to include love in your words. When you don't write or talk anymore, then I will know you're tired of loving people. I have always bound the necks of hatred, but I'm tired of doing it for you. Some of you feel at peace because you're miles away from conflict. I still want you to walk the miles and feel the pain of others. I desire only peace, love, and harmony for you.

Do you understand love? Do you know love? These are questions that will cause you to either survive or die. I love you, but I will still judge you. I judge you as individuals, as if you were numbers. No one is better than anyone else. You are small to me compared to other things I have created. You must take my words and comprehend them. You must understand my love for you. You must love others. If you do not, your tears will continue to be salty, and love will sleep.

OCTOBER 13, 2014: JESUS STILL LOVED HIS BETRAYER

Jesus still loved his betrayer. Jesus never said at the Last Supper that he would discriminate as to who could receive communion. He only wanted you to eat in remembrance of him. Jesus forgave Judas, the betrayer. Judas took the Eucharist as well. Jesus knew there was a betrayer and still allowed the Eucharist to be shared by all at the table. Please don't misinterpret my word, for it's the same message for all.

Come as one. Think as one. See as one. Feel as one. Love as one. Be humble, and don't discriminate. I freed the slaves of Egypt from bondage, and I will free you from militants, haters, and false caliphates. The lesson of slavery is to remind you that nothing awaits discriminatory hearts that continue to hate. Your focus as humans is destructive and contrasts with my intentions. Remember, Jesus still loved his betrayer.

OCTOBER 16, 2014: COOPERATION

Cooperation will create the ability to sustain international collaboration. America and Africa must collaborate. It will create a massive step for humankind. It will be higher than the walk on the moon. It will contain a pandemic. Let's not forget that the plague killed at least one-third of the population of Europe, but the human race still survived. The virus exists in rats today, but we experience no significant threat from the disease.

People worried the Black Death would destroy the human race for good, but we have more people now than ever before. More people will die if you continue to hate. It's time for all races and religions to work together. Today there are worse diseases than the plague.

Imagine what people from long ago would think about today's technology. So many women and children died in childbirth without technology. We must advance in the medical industry, especially in the field of the apothecary. Don't fear progressiveness. Fear not; walk out of your house with a sense of unity in your heart. If everyone walked out of their homes with love in their hearts, the isolation of fear would be over. Communication would thrive, and respect for each other would connect us again.

If you ask about the future without collaboration, I can't yet answer. I leave it up to you. Every prayer I hear I hear collectively from everybody without discrimination or denominations! It's part of the reason you're still here, that I have not splattered your sun and stars or burned you to ashes.

Hateful minds on earth that only seeking prosperity will go to nothing. If you hate those who are despised, then you're guilty too. If you hold those hated accountable and punish them accordingly, that's righteous. The criminal can still be forgiven or held liable just as the murderer Cain was punished. The fears you have today will destroy the happiness of tomorrow if you're not strong enough to walk out of your houses and love each other.

OCTOBER 16, 2014: A PRAYER FOR SAVING

Please don't destroy us for our transgressions. There's still one, two, or more of us that will carry on beliefs that you've taught. When your volcano erupts, please don't swallow me in your lava. Please save me. Put me higher, where my feet won't burn. But only put me higher if you feel that I'm worthy.

OCTOBER 16, 2014: DISEASES

Ebola is a warning! Ebola is a punishment for the mistreatment of and lack of respect for women and children. Those who are willing to help are those who will save others. If people are unwilling to save others and help each other, then we're no longer relying on ourselves for help. Those who volunteer to help in a crisis are as heroic as those who fight to protect their families. The family is the human race. Don't forget other diseases—polio, HIV, AIDS, chicken pox, measles, and herpes. All of these diseases have been controlled and serve as a warning.

OCTOBER 16, 2014: PACIFY HATRED

We shall not ignore the people who need us! Although that command won't stand because some of you allow people to starve, freeze in the street, or even be killed in the desert. But one day a group of five leaders will climb and meet on a mountain! They'll be of different colors, races, and beliefs. Every language is different, but every heart is the same. They'll agree on everything. They'll eat together and share food. They'll laugh at all hatred toward others. Finally they'll answer all the questions and pacify *hatred!*

OCTOBER 16, 2014: ONE GOOD PERSON

The plagues that your Lord put upon Egypt caused pain and suffering, yet Egypt still exists today. People still live, even though pestilence and all of the much deserved horrors were prevalent. Why? For what good reason? I will tell you. There were more good people than bad people. So I saved the good ones and drowned the bad. Unfortunately modern people have a lack of understanding and compassion for each other again. I must keep a certain percentage of the bad population and hope the remaining portion of the good population will stand up for righteousness.

Better yet, if there's one good person in a town of bad people, that one person will be brought to the town's attention. Then more people will recognize what's good and choose the right path. Ask yourself why there are still towns and countries in the modern world without running water. Advanced technology should have solved this problem. Why are people dying of typhoid? How many more years will it take for this suffering to stop? Only the human race can answer these questions because it's up to you now.

I gave you the technology and resources, but you don't share them with poor people. Corrupt governments that don't care about their constituents can answer that question, but you won't get a truthful answer from them.

    Cooperation is the key to the future! Confronted with world tragedies, what other choice do humans have? Murder, killing, raping, and abusing are *not* the way.

OCTOBER 17, 2014: A HOUSE OF GOLD

There once was a house of gold, and the family that lived there treated each other with respect, but the husband and wife never really married for the right reasons. Therefore they had disdain for each other as the years went on. Their children recognized this and realized that all of their gold was worthless. So they agreed to exchange their house of gold for a tent because they yearned for love from their parents. In their minds, the weight of love had more intrinsic value than any metal.

Love is worth more than gold and knows no distance either. Long stretches of the ocean can't stop the constant thought about and yearning to be with someone when you're in love. No matter how far apart you are, no matter how many years apart, love will last. There's no distance that love can't traverse. We all feel the same pain within us. How we express that pain makes a difference in how we treat each other. There's only one thing everyone should hate—hate.

OCTOBER 27, 2014: KARMA OF BAD LOVERS

Bad lovers wallow in themselves. Karma will eventually catch up with them. They are miserable because they don't know how to treat other people with respect and love, especially those who love them the most.

NOVEMBER 29, 2014: KNOW THE BEATITUDES

You must love unconditionally. Be it your father, mother, brother, sister, son, or daughter. A lot of death is coming because of our hatred for the race and color of others. Combat it with love and righteousness. If you want to stop hate, take a rotten heart and replace it with a good one.

The less intelligent will be armed, and the more intelligent won't be loaded. However the smart will win. Eventually the ones who have power will be intellectuals because their technology will evolve beyond guns and explosives. Righteousness will win. Don't worry.

Once again, humans will force each other into a battle over insignificant hatred, and that will be on the side of those who already project hatred and make it visible. There's one horrible thing that will happen again: many people will die for both parties. Only some will see the floating heart. The ones who see the floating heart will win the war. There will be a great sacrifice, but righteousness is worth death. There'll be a place in the light for those who die for righteousness.

If your heart pumps blood in your veins, there's no reason to deny love. People who have bad intentions are denying love even unto themselves. You know, the heart exists in the mind, and your mind controls your heart. Every house of worship needs to recite the beatitudes. No one can deny them, for you know they're right.

Read the beatitudes over and over until you know them by heart. If you don't believe in them, you won't be sanctified and forgiven. The beatitudes stand for all religions across the world! If you don't follow them, then you don't deserve communion. Now you can take it, but you're only serving yourself.

Don't believe any iteration of the beatitudes that doesn't start with "Blessed are." The beatitudes stand for the heart of humanity. The Eucharist is not holy if you don't know the beatitudes. If you don't know them, think twice before you take communion; you should know them by heart. If you don't know them, then don't take communion.

Know the beatitudes, and stop the hate. Love is absent now. There's still time to memorize and study them. When you're knowledgeable about what they mean, then you will understand the Eucharist and stop taking it out of habit. Once you know the beatitudes, hatred will end.

DECEMBER 4, 2014: THE PATH TO TRUE HAPPINESS

Memorize the Ten Commandments as well as the Beatitudes that Jesus taught as a path to true happiness. Saint Francis of Assisi was so serious about reciting the beatitudes that he would recite them over and over. There's a spell cast over the Ten Commandments and eight beatitudes. The spell makes it hard to remember them. It would be best if you overcame it. Recite them one hundred times and study them if you want to break the spell.

Many priests and monks have broken the spell because they continuously recite and study them. Unfortunately the average person doesn't examine the Ten Commandments and eight beatitudes. If you don't believe me, name them. I bet many of you can't recite more than two. If you want to overcome the spell of hate and find true happiness, you must continue to recite them over and over until you have memorized them. Never stop studying the Ten Commandments and eight beatitudes if you want to continue to feel loved. I have made things this way on purpose.

DECEMBER 19, 2014: FEEL THE BLIGHT OF CAIN

You may feel satisfied with everything you have right now. However Jesus suffered forty days and forty nights for you. If you don't love others for who they are, you can never feel loved for who you are. Put family before evil. This includes your father, mother, brothers, sisters—all. The one who loves his wife is the one who loves the most. Don't neglect children. They need you the most.

When I touched the hand of Adam, I felt humanity of a form I desired for you. When I touched Cain, I hated him. I still gave him a free choice, even though he blighted me. You're a citizen of Cain, and you'll feel my blight too. You can kill your brother, run, and hide, but you can never escape me because I know everything. I, not you, pick who you are.

No one face is more beautiful to me than another. In the same respect, all your faces are beautiful to me. Accept each other because you're created equal in my eyes! We're close to turmoil, and I'll let your pestilence destroy you. In the end, I'm still the parent, and you're my children.

JANUARY 1, 2015: COMPROMISE-BASED SOLUTIONS

In order to get along, the people of the world must have respect and love; compromise-based solutions will save us from an unnecessary revolution. If you don't love anyone but yourself, can you love anyone? That is an example of selfishness. Do you feed the poor, or do you only feed yourself? Both need food. When you pass people in a crowd and they smile at you and you don't smile back, you're arrogant.

Travel down a long road, through a path, over hills and dales. You'll come to a village. The people in this town accept and take you into their homes. They don't care what color and race you are. They see you as an equal. How do you feel? You enjoy your stay there, and they're hospitable. When you leave, ask yourself, *Have I ever been treated any better by people whom I don't see as equal?*

JANUARY 12, 2015: WALK THE MOUNT OF BEATITUDES

Walk the Mount of Beatitudes. It resembles the same shape and form as that mount where Jesus taught the beatitudes during his Sermon on the Mount. Recite them. Then look out at the terrain and think about the multitude of listeners and the beautiful words that Jesus spoke. Again, the mount is still there. You have left it, but it hasn't left you.

The mount exists in every house, too, and the beatitudes are the same. If you study and know them, you can still visit the Mount of Beatitudes in your mind with your family. You don't have to make a pilgrimage and walk the footpath to experience it. Instead draw your heart close to the mount. Imagine walking there, even though your feet aren't touching the dirt and gravel. Most of you have left the mount, but it's still there.

MAY 29, 2015: GIFTS TO INSPIRE THE WORLD

Disease and famine are gifts to inspire the world to advance and draw humans closer to one another through cooperation. Those who interpret them otherwise and fail to participate are bitter of heart and soul. They're blinded but can be cured. Bitterness is only an ailment of itself.

MAY 29, 2015: EQUALITY FOR ALL

Equality will exist for all upon humanity's recognition of its inequality with God. *I am.*

MAY 29, 2015: TRUE LEADERS

Corrupt rulers cause the ultimate destruction and demise of their people. True, righteous leaders of humankind bring about peace and prosperity. Find me a ruler who has lasted for ages, for the right leaders and thinkers of humanity are timeless and never stop leading, even after death.

JULY 16, 2015: EXPOSE CORRUPTION

The leaders of the church are closest to God. So they must speak out against evil and expose the sins of the church. If they do not, the leaders are causing more harm to the world than are any other individuals. The leaders of the church are the authority, the ones everyone entrusts with their faith and the ability to directly communicate with me. If they don't speak out against the sins of the church, I will cease speaking to them.

By not speaking out against evil, leaders of the church are committing the ultimate crime against God. Let their silence expose their evil hearts; they can't hide corruption from me under their cloaks. They've lost their faith. They're nothing to me now. Let it be known that if you take communion from faithless leaders of the church, the Eucharist does not work. Now they are brothers of Satan.

Leaders of the church must not fear backlash for exposing the sins of the church. The backlash is nothing more than the sins of thought boiling to the surface. The leaders are now letting their evil hearts hold them back and committing sins of greater magnitude. It's the same for vipers in church. Don't go to church, listen to a sermon about love, and then allow children to be hurt. You wound the Lamb of God when you hide the sins of the church. Instead you must rush out and expose the crimes of the church.

Leaders of the church who do not expose evil are hypocritical because everyone knows the difference between good and evil. The victims don't come forward because they are afraid of the backlash. It would be best if everyone supported the victims and stopped ignoring the sin. It's selfish not to help the victims. They are just trying to do the right thing. Try to remember, forgiveness does not exclude consequences.

Now be warned—some leaders of the church seek pleasure in suffering instead of compassion! Some people are born with a mental defect because sometimes things go wrong in the physical makeup of a human being. It's harder to penetrate their hearts with truth because they're not remorseful. They seek pleasure from heinous acts. They're not exploring the beauty in the sky, water, and flowers. Instead they find twisted pleasure in the reverse of love.

Happy-sad. Sad-happy. We can pray for them, but sometimes we can't stop evil. Within the bigger picture, their sins show others how to not be like them. Is there hope for them? There's always hope for the world, but it doesn't follow them. All bad things going on in the church should help reform the church.

All religious leaders must expose the corruption of their places of worship, which includes sexism and prejudice. These unfortunate examples show people you're not on the right path to God and need to purge the evil from the church first and foremost. The day a leader of the church accepts women as priests, people will leave the church, but accepting women will save the church by inviting in real believers! The leaders of the church must lead by these examples.

JULY 16, 2015: COLLECTIVE HEART OF LOVE

The world has to be a collective heart of love and cleanse itself of hate. All symbols of hatred must fall, including signs, slogans, and statues. Everyone knows particular flags are offensive to people who suffered under the tyranny they represent. So these flags must fall too. Change is difficult when you believe the lies told to you, but people will prevail at bringing down hate. Those who don't care won't prevail. If better hearts exist on Earth, life will balance again. The world must purge itself of toxins such as selfishness, greed, hate, sexism, and prejudice.

Right now, in America, some people are following hate. The leader of the free world is stirring up hatred and toxins in people. People with fear in their hearts will be vulnerable to these hateful toxins, but don't worry. When the dirty water comes to the top, the wrong intentions of this leader will be exposed. Then he'll fall, too, just like the symbols of hatred. We can't allow other countries to follow his example. I'm letting this happen so my people overcome hate and accept love in their hearts again.

DECEMBER 14, 2016: ALEPPO WAS A WARNING

I'm on the verge of destroying Earth again because you're warping my words of love with hate. This time I won't stop the destruction. The process has already begun because there are less than good people again. Is it too late? The end has already happened for the people of Aleppo. I have chosen that place to be the epicenter of denial because it serves as a warning that will go unheeded.

To a little girl in Aleppo, today was the end of the world, and you didn't care. Her tweets and photos were a warning to a corrupt society that hasn't learned from its past transgressions. Picture the Earth as a person. The aura surrounding the land is evil now. Create a world that has a positive energy that's worthy of reward rather than punishment.

Evil is mistaken for good and good misunderstood as sin. Things have gone awry—the desire for wealth and prosperity is stronger than the regard for love and humanity. People are crying for help, and you turn your hearts away. The salt in their tears is quickly evaporating due to the fire of hatred. Love is the only answer. Are you listening?

DECEMBER 14, 2016: LOVE EACH OTHER EQUALLY

Until about fifty years ago, countries still had discriminatory laws. This means hate has dictated the majority of the world population's thought processes over the course of evolution. It proves you're still a corrupt and hateful world. You have been around for thousands of years, but *only* about fifty years ago you began trying to love each other equally. Now hate is winning again. That was a short run, considering the time you've been on earth. How easily you dismiss your history.

Learn to love each other equally, and I will grant humans access to the complexities of the universe. Unfortunately humans continue to spread corruption. So I have made time travel forbidden for you now. I won't allow humans to murder beyond your realm. Consider yourself contained until further notice. Why do you think other species haven't destroyed you yet? If murder and corruption were allowed to spread throughout the universe, you wouldn't exist.

Any form of hate and self-destruction enacts the law of forbidden space travel. So your math has become temporarily useless. That's why your scientists can't formulate a breakthrough, no matter how hard they try. Unfortunately you'll not live to reach another star. I won't allow it. I gave you the knowledge and skills, but I have retracted them.

Release your containment of hate, and I will allow time travel. Only then will I allow you to meet others that have overcome hatred too. Until then I will instead let you be destroyed by your hand, after which I destroy those who have overcome hate. I need to preserve harmony in the heavens. When advancement of your psychology and humanity takes precedence over that of your astronomy and physics, you will become closer to the key that will release your containment. Forget speed. Space travel exists in your collective consciousness.

DECEMBER 31, 2016: TRUE CHANNELS

If one can remember the channel without an apostle witness, it's not a real channel. Without loss of recollection, the words are false. Truth from the unknown takes the power of human energy from the conduit. So there must be a witness. The conduit is not allowed to remember. A witness must pass on the words. Those who witnessed but altered the truth are not pure of heart.

Altering the truth from a channel is evil and selfish. Now falsehoods are passed on to generations who adopt and believe these falsehoods as truths. Now the disease of evil has embedded itself in the fabric of humanity. Those genuinely seeking the light are being led by the misinformed. Look not to those figures who preach what appears to be the truth, for they don't know the truth.

The desolate and desperate have more knowledge of the truth than those who appear to know it. Listen to them. They're more informed than the ones in the position to teach it, for the teachers are misinformed. The suffering and desolate are showing the world a lesson of truth, but the classroom is still barren. Falsehoods have corrupted the learning process.

JANUARY 21, 2017: THE FACE OF GOD

Don't ask me to see me because God has no face. God has no flesh. God is a skull, but there's a swarm of energy inside of me. It swirls with green, purple, red, and orange, like a hologram. Still, if you were to see my face, you would look away in fear. Yes, I created people in my image, but I have no covering. Humans have flesh, but I don't have flesh. I made you beautiful by giving you flesh. You're a solid form of God but have a covering. Everyone wants to see me, but you would be scared to see what's under your flesh because there's no beauty.

God may be ugly, but what God does is beautiful. Remember that. God's image is nonphysical. God exists inside of his head and doesn't exist too. There's no space and time for God. It's a state of being that humans cannot conceive. There are swirling colors in the head of God's hologram—colors you don't know exist, so you don't recognize them yet. You're a created art form of me. So please don't ask my name or to see me. I need no title and no face. But I'm here for you.

… FROM GOD, FOR YOU AND ME

PARABLE ONE: A WOMAN SITS ALONE

D. L. and I found a woman crying on a bench after we left a restaurant. We stopped to check on her, and she told us about losing her son to drug addiction. Spirit sent her to us as a test of compassion.

—M.

A woman is sitting alone on a wooden bench. She's desperately waiting for someone. So I sit beside her.

"Have you seen my son?" she asks with worry.

"No, I haven't," I reply.

She swallows her tears and keeps looking out into the parking lot for her son. She's frantic now.

"What happened?" I ask.

"My son suffered permanent brain injuries after his car accident. Now he's addicted to drugs, homeless, and angry. He's supposed to meet me here. Have you seen my son?" The woman shares her story.

"No, I'm so sorry," I reply. "What's your name?"

"Barbara. I'm his mother," she cries.

I hold the woman's hand and listen to her tears of sorrow. Her son is lost, but she's not alone.

PARABLE TWO: THE MAN WITH A CANE

D. L. went out for a few errands and returned to our apartment with horror on his face. He just witnessed a man with a cane fall on the street, and he was the only one that stopped to help him. A few minutes later, I received this message from Spirit, and it was on fire.

—M.

The man with a cane fell on the street, and no one stopped to help him up. When the man with a cane fell on the road, the world descended on the street. Do you feel my anger and sadness now? The man represents the truth of lost compassion that people have for the world because nobody even turned his or her head. There were many witnesses, but nobody felt love enough in their hearts to help the man with the cane.

How many people have witnessed a poor, old, and disabled man fall in the street, yet still done nothing to help him? They ignore the man with a cane. I am covering my face and crying for you. The sadness that I feel is over your lack of love for humanity. If people don't understand the pain this man felt, then you don't understand the pain my son felt for you. You pretend, but you don't.

Tell the story of this man. My son would have asked you to

provide shelter, wash, house, feed, water, console, and sacrifice for him. Let the people that passed by this man be heathens on display. They know what they did. They saw the man with the cane fall on the street, and they still ignored him. They did not rescue him. They put themselves *before* the man with the cane!

Selfishness is a horror. Let's ask the people what they would want from me if they were the man who fell in the street. Now you wonder why I'm so sad and angry. Let the story of the man with a cane be a lesson in the event you should fall. Should I pick you up if you have broken your hips? You're nothing before me, and *I am* your cane. Don't go before the alter until you feel compassion and understanding for the person in this story. Otherwise your beliefs before the altar are false.

Your lack of love for the man with a cane makes me want to smash your bones because I detest fakers. Those who didn't stop for the man won't see me after they have passed through Death. Is this what you want? I don't want this book to be about not seeing me. Have you missed the meaning of this story? Have you lost the lessons on love? People—priests, preachers, rabbis, and prophets—tried to explain these simple acts of love, but you still passed by the man with the cane.

When I come to see you for the last time, you'll understand everything I have said. If you don't, I'll have no choice but to judge you for good. Choose your judgment, but *I am* the judge. Your passing by the man with the cane has backed me into a corner because I have lost patience. There's more hate than love in my world now. I may have to take back my love for the world because you make me so sad.

You need to walk a mile in the shoes of the man with a cane. Don't you know who *I am*? Go to an infirmary and think about others. Go to a place of suffering and think about me. You haven't read enough. If you haven't read, you haven't felt. But if you have read and felt, then you will go out of your way to treat others as I have commanded you to do.

FROM GOD, FOR YOU AND ME

A PERSONAL ESSAY FROM DEATH

I found D. L. sitting with his back against the wall, shouting down the hallway by his father's bedroom, and daring someone to a fight. I looked and saw Death emerge, like a big mouth of darkness.

—M.

I am Death, and I have one task. I'm the acceptor of all things that have passed. People shudder with fright when confronted by my doomed shadow, but I'm not evil. The families of the ill even dare to fight me because they mistake me for a murderer. Other guilty souls beg me for forgiveness, but I offer no closure or compassion. So please do not ask me for mercy because I'm merely a doorway to the other side. I'm a servant of God. Reveal my truth. That's all I ask of you.

Death lives inside an eternal cage by the nature of God's creation. Do you want to know what happens after your last breath? Do you want to know what happens after your soul passes through me? I'm unable to answer these questions because I'm forbidden to see as you're forbidden to know. I only chose to tell you these things because you talk to beings that God hasn't taken yet. Spirits are not of my ruin either. I see them, but they don't come through me. They have done something the creator isn't pleased with, but one day all will pass through me.

Death exists, but consciousness is my only creation. I take life, but I don't kill. Death is the original gray creation, like no human or angel. Only humans have colors, race, and hatred for each other. You anger me by bringing me into the light of the sun. So let me go back into the darkness. Put your images of me away. Death is not just ink on paper.

CONCLUSION

From God, for You and Me: Angelic Dreams and Supernatural Encounters is also not just ink on paper. Let these messages provide hope and inspiration for everyone. My goals in publishing this book are to enhance your spirituality, give ways of restoring love for humanity, and share my story, which continues to this day. After spirit communication with D. L. ended in 2017, I started to receive divine messages from the other side. You may read about them in my second book, *Angels in Arms: Words of Love, Strength, and Protection*. I hope you will continue to listen.

Angel by D.L.

The Divine Light by D.L.

Angel Energy by D.L.

FROM GOD, FOR YOU AND ME

ABOUT THE AUTHOR

Monique A. Everett was born and raised in Jim Thorpe, Pennsylvania. She holds a Master of Education Degree and School Library and Information Technologies from Mansfield University as well as a Bachelor of Science in Education and Library Science from Kutztown University. Monique has been a teacher-librarian for over two decades. She is also a Reiki Master and provides energy healing, property cleansing, and spiritual mentorship for family, friends, and coworkers. Monique is very active on social media and will answer questions regarding her books. Visit her blog, artwork, and additional titles at www.moniqueeverett.com.

www.ingramcontent.com/pod-product-compliance
Lightning Source LLC
LaVergne TN
LVHW090116080426
835507LV00040B/956